FIRE ENGINES
OF
NORTH EAST
ENGLAND

Ron Henderson

Nostalgia Road Publications

CONTENTS

The **Nostalgia Road** Series ™

is produced under licence by

Nostalgia Road Publications Ltd.

Units 5 - 8, Chancel Place,

Shap Road Industrial Estate,

Kendal, Cumbria, LA9 6NZ

Tel. +44 (0)1539 738832 - Fax: +44 (0)1539 730075

designed and published by

Trans-Pennine Publishing Ltd.

PO Box 10, Appleby-in-Westmorland, Cumbria, CA16 6FA
Tel. +44 (0)17683 51053 Fax. +44 (0)17683 53558
e-mail: admin@transpenninepublishing.co.uk

and printed by

Kent Valley Colour Printers Ltd.

Kendal, Cumbria - +44 (0)1539 741344

Front Cover: *One of Tyne & Wear's classic Dennis F131 pumps is seen here at a disused school fire at Jarrow in April 1980. In the background is former South Shields Fire Brigade AEC turntable ladder.*

Rear Cover Top: *One of the former Newcastle and Gateshead Fire Services AEC-Merryweather turntable ladders in operation as a water tower at Vickers Armstrongs Factory, Scotswood Road Newcastle in July 1980.*

Rear Cover Bottom: *Tyne & Wear operated three Dennis DF133 turntable ladders with German Magirus ladders. Gateshead's example is pictured in October 1986 at a major cash and carry warehouse fire in Durham's area.*

Title Page: *Darlington Fire Brigade's first post-war delivery was a Whitson-bodied Commer water tender, which is pictured here at a farm fire shortly after delivery.* B. Clayton collection

This Page: *This photograph illustrates the wide array of ladders that was carried on Northumberland's Commer-Miles multi purpose pumps. The wheeled escape was a 50ft Bayley model and was supplemented by a short extension ladder, hook ladder and 35ft extension ladder.*

ISBN 1 903016 67 3
British Cataloguing in Publication Data
A catalogue record for this book is available from the British Library

INTRODUCTION

This book sets out to describe the fire appliances that have operated within the local authority fire brigades of the north east of England in the counties of Cleveland, Durham, Northumberland and Tyne and Wear. The constraints of the book versus the amount of appliances do not allow for every type of appliance to be described or illustrated and therefore the material concentrates on the vehicles that have been in use from the end of World War II up to the present day, most of which will still be within the realms of the reader's memory.

As well as describing the equipment of the four large county brigades of today, it also describes the appliances of the constituent brigades that were in existence before the big local authority merger of 1974.

Above: *Both of Newcastle & Gateshead Fire Service's pre-war Leyland turntable ladders and a Bedford salvage tender are seen in action in Northumberland Street, Newcastle in the 1960s.* Newcastle Chronicle and Journal

This merger resulted in the formation of larger fire authorities with bigger fleets signalling the introduction of a great degree of standardisation, particularly as far as pumping appliances are concerned. This is in contrast to the many smaller brigades that existed before the merger, where individual local risks and boundaries provided for much specialisation and variation in fire appliance types. The illustrations featured range from examples of the standard types commonly seen, to some of the more unusual and unique vehicles that have operated in the four counties since the nationalised fire services disbanded in 1948.

CLEVELAND FIRE BRIGADE

MIDDLESBROUGH FIRE BRIGADE

Middlesbrough Fire Brigade commenced its post-war existence with two fire stations and a total of eleven appliances, three of them pre-war Borough machines consisting of two Leyland pumps and a Leyland turntable ladder. The remainder consisted of an assortment of wartime standard fire appliances. There was also an estuarial type fireboat 'on the strength' berthed at the marine fire station adjacent to the Transporter Bridge. During its post-war existence, the brigade only purchased six new fire engines but amongst them were some most unusual examples.

Above: *This unusual Leyland lighting unit was a former pump escape, originally named* Sir Samuel Sadler, *delivered to Middlesbrough in 1936. In 1959 it was converted into its new role by the Brigade's workshop personnel.* Ian Moore

The first new appliance to be purchased by Middlesbrough, was a Home Office allocated Rolls Royce powered Dennis F7 limousine appliance complete with wheeled escape, which was chosen following visits by members of the Fire Brigade Committee to the manufacturers works at Guildford and East Ham Fire Brigade (near London) that had received the prototype. Delivered three days before Christmas 1950 it was followed two years later by a second Home Office allocation, a major pumping appliance.

This was based on a normal control Leyland Comet chassis with Windover bodywork, which was considered a fine acquisition. Two years after delivery, the appliance was fitted with a larger, 400-gallons water tank for dealing with calls to the rural outskirts of Middlesbrough. Serving the town until 1969 it was one of only three of this type to see service in the north-east, the other two operating with Durham County Fire Brigade. The Brigade's third new delivery was another Dennis appliance, an F12 series machine, similar to the earlier F7 but with a reduced wheelbase. This appliance was unusual in the fact that the registration number, DDC 1 was still being used on fire appliances in 2005, having been transferred to successive new appliances of Cleveland Fire Brigade.

In 1956, the Brigade took delivery of an appliance that will go down in the annals of history as being one of the most unusual appliances ever built. Prompted by headroom constraints on the route into Middlesbrough Docks, a pre-war open-top Leyland had sufficed but the imminent replacement required an equally low height type of appliance. With specifications requiring a maximum ceiling height of 7ft, Dennis Bros of Guildford came up with an appropriate design. The result, based on a Dennis F12 chassis, revealed an open-topped 400 gallons water tender with the driver sitting in his own single cab, in a manner similar to many buses. The appliance featured a rear-mounted 500gpm pump and carried the standard array of ladders, stowed horizontally along the insides of the body. Apart from the red-painted front the remainder of the appliance was finished in unpainted embossed aluminium, the first such appliance in the north-east.

Top Right: *There were few, if any post-war fire Brigades that did not inherit one of these National Fire Service 'heavy unit' appliances. This one, mounted onto a Bedford chassis was assigned to Middlesbrough Fire Brigade and accompanies a multitude of other types at a Civil Defence exercise in 1952.*

Middle Right: *The second post-war delivery to Middlesbrough was this smart Leyland Comet major pump, pictured in 1967. Two similar appliances were delivered to Durham County Fire Brigade. For some reason the ladder is stowed at a very acute angle.* Ian Moore

Bottom Right: *The unique half-cab Dennis F12 water tender of Middlesbrough Fire Brigade is pictured turning out to a fire in 1969. The fibreglass roof was a later addition on what was originally an open-topped appliance.*

Ever-conscious of the fact that having firemen exposed to the elements was a retrograde step, in 1959 the machine was fitted with a fibreglass roof that could be easily removed in the event of a call being received to the docks. The unique appliance later passed to a Stockton timber merchant as a works fire appliance and has fortunately since been acquired for preservation. Two further appliances were ordered before the Brigade was absorbed into the new Teesside County Fire Brigade in 1968.

In 1962 one of Merryweather's successful hydraulic turntable ladders on the AEC Mercury chassis was delivered, and this gave the region excellent value as the ladder equipment was later remounted onto a new Dennis chassis by Cleveland Fire Brigade. Middlesbrough's final delivery was another unique combination for the north-east, a Bedford TK emergency tender with bodywork by Dennis M; the 'M' signifying it was of Alfred Miles pedigree, Miles being a prolific builder of fire engines that had recently merged with Dennis Bros.

This appliance replaced another unusual appliance, a surplus Leyland Braidwood motor pump that had been converted in 1959 by workshops personnel into an emergency lighting unit using a secondhand 3kw generator. This was later removed and relocated to the headquarters station basement for use as an alternative energy source in the event of an electrical mains failure. The Brigade did operate other appliances, mostly conversions of former National Fire Service (NFS) vehicles, some of which fulfiled the roles of emergency tender and foam tender until more suitable equipment became available. On 1st April 1968, Middlesbrough Fire Brigade lost its identity and became incorporated into Teesside County Fire Brigade.

Below: *In 1965 Middlesbrough took delivery of this Bedford TK emergency tender with coachwork by Dennis M. It was the last appliance to be ordered by the Brigade before it was encompassed into Teesside in 1968.* Ian Moore

This Brigade operated from one fire station until 1967 but in common with most small Brigades it had an interesting array of appliances. One appliance inherited in 1948, was the town's pre-war Leyland FKT limousine motor pump but the remainder were ex-NFS appliances, including a 100ft Merryweather turntable ladder on a Leyland Beaver chassis. The first new appliance was a Dennis F12 pump escape, and the next to be delivered was also a Dennis, one of the F8 series, which was fitted with an Alfred Miles body. The third delivery was also from Dennis and was one of the latest F20 series dual- purpose appliances equipped to carry the Brigade's wheeled escape.

A Bedford-Miles emergency unit was delivered in 1962, similar to a pair already in service in Durham, the Hartlepool appliance advertised its role as a rescue tender by the attachment of a full width black panel on the roof front displaying the legend 'Accident Vehicle' in orange. In 1966 an AEC Mercury Merryweather 100ft turntable ladder replaced the wartime Leyland and in 1968 an interesting Bedford TK pump hydraulic platform was delivered.

In 1967, Durham County Fire Brigade's Hartlepool Headland station was incorporated into the West Hartlepool fleet to form the Hartlepool Fire Brigade. A Commer Miles water tender and a Bedford Miles water tender were inherited during the merger. The last appliance to be purchased by the Borough was a rare Carmichael-bodied Leyland Lynx water tender/ladder, which was delivered in 1971. The Brigade never operated a custom-built foam tender; instead the matter was addressed by the purchase of a BMC FG type drop-side lorry to carry foam.

The appliances that served in Hartlepool were readily identifiable by their Day-Glo orange bumpers and uniquely; each machine was adorned with the Chief Fire Officer's name painted on the side. The new, enlarged Brigade only had a short life span for in 1974 another merger took place and Hartlepool Brigade was incorporated into the new County of Cleveland.

Top Right: *Northumberland, Durham and Hartlepool fire brigades all operated examples of the Miles-bodied Dennis F8. Pictured here in 1970 is the sole Hartlepool example.* Ian Moore

Middle Right: *Delivered in 1962, West Hartlepool's Bedford/Miles emergency tender acquired a white front after being incorporated into the Cleveland fleet in 1974.*

Bottom Right: *This Leyland Lynx dating from 1971 was the last appliance to be issued to Hartlepool Fire Brigade.* Ian Moore

TEESSIDE FIRE BRIGADE

This Brigade was formed on 1st April 1968 and commenced with a total of 19 assorted fire engines inherited through an amalgamation of brigades and fire stations from Hartlepool, Middlesbrough, Durham County (Stockton), and the North Riding of Yorkshire (Grangetown, Redcar and Thornaby). With just six stations and one in build at Billingham it was one of the smallest County Brigades in the country. Its existence was notably short lived for just six years after its formation another merger saw the County of Teesside disappear.

The inherited North Riding appliances totalled seven, one Dennis F12 pump escape at Grangetown and six HCB-bodied Bedford's of assorted types including a custom built HCB-Angus foam tender. From Durham came five appliances, the oldest a Commer Miles foam carrier dating from 1952 that had been a water tender before undergoing a conversion by Durham County Fire Brigade.

Above: *Devoid of any identification, this former North Riding of Yorkshire Fire Brigade Bedford/HCB water tender was one of several that passed into Teesside in 1968. The only clue to its Teesside ownership is the fleet number just behind the indicator light.*

To supplement the fleet during the first year three Green Goddesses (from the Auxiliary Fire Service) and a Ford Thames signals van (from the Civil Defence) were bought from the Home Office, the latter for conversion into a mobile control unit. The first new appliances ordered by the embryo brigade were based on AEC TGM chassis and totalled seven in all with bodies constructed by the big three of the day, Carmichael, HCB-Angus and Merryweather.

Two of the batch were foam tankers equipped with facilities for towing large Merryweather 'Major' dual-purpose foam monitors, for use in cases of fire at the developing petro-chemical complexes that by then lined the River Tees.

All subsequent deliveries during the remainder of the Brigade's short existence were based on Dennis vehicle chassis, mainly F108 series appliances and consisted of six pumps and one emergency tender; the latter being substantially rebuilt as the prototype for the emergency tender of the future, the *Cleveland*. This development, which was claimed to be "not the usual inadequate adaptation of standard vehicles" was designed by an interesting partnership. This was comprised of the Brigade and Teesside Polytechnic, and had financial support from the County Council and the Manpower Services Commission. Visually, the prototype bore no resemblance to the first and only operational development that was later placed into service by Cleveland County Fire Brigade.

One high-rise appliance was delivered in 1973 on a Dennis F123 chassis with a Simon 85ft hydraulic platform. It was followed by two Dennis F108 water tenders by which time, after only six years of existence, the Brigade was subsumed by the newly created Cleveland County Fire Brigade, relegating Teesside Fire Brigade to the history books as quick as it was founded.

During its short existence the Brigade introduced the white fronts to the appliance fleet, commencing with Stockton's Bedford water tender, which had the rear portion of the roof painted white. The first new appliance to be delivered with the new livery was Billingham's first AEC/HCB-Angus water tender/ladder. Thereafter most of the Teesside fleet and all deliveries to Cleveland Fire Brigade continued to maintain this unusual characteristic.

Top Right: *One North Riding of Yorkshire Dennis F12 was inherited by the Teesside Fire Brigade upon its formation in 1968. Based at Grangetown the appliance is pictured at a house fire shortly after the merger.*

Middle Right: *The Teesside fleet was supplemented by a number of secondhand Green Goddess appliances, acquired after the disbanding of the illustrious Auxiliary Fire Service in 1968. Pictured is a 4x4 version on standby at Teesside Airport in 1969.*

Bottom Right: *The first new appliances acquired by Teesside comprised of batches of AECs. This HCB-Angus water tender ladder was pictured at Billingham in 1971, shortly after the station opened and was the first new delivery to feature the white cab and roof. Teesside was still specifying the fitting of bells at this late stage.*

CLEVELAND FIRE BRIGADE

The Local Government Re-organisation Act, implemented in 1974 saw the amalgamation of Hartlepool and Teesside Brigades with North Riding of Yorkshire's Guisborough, Loftus, Saltburn, Skelton and Yarm part-time fire stations. This resulted in the formation of a new County containing contrasting areas of heavy industrialisation surrounding the River Tees, and predominantly rural aspects bordering the restructured County of North Yorkshire. All the North Riding appliances were Bedford water tenders with unpainted aluminium bodies with the exception of Saltburn's appliance which was equipped with a 60ft Merryweather steel escape in view of the numerous hotels and boarding houses in the seaside town. This wheeled escape was the last one to be withdrawn from any of the brigades covered in this history.

Above: *Carrying the registration plates from a former Middlesbrough Dennis major pump, DDC 1 is seen at Stockton in 1976, when brand new and before the white fronts became a universal feature on the Brigade's appliances. The number plates were again later transferred onto the vehicle's replacement appliance.*

The appliance fleet of Cleveland County Fire Brigade, certainly as far as pumps were concerned, was predominantly of Dennis origin after an initial batch of three Carmichael-bodied Dodge K850 water tenders were ordered. The first Dennis of the new Brigade was a Dennis F123 Simon Snorkel appliance, which was retro-fitted with the number plate from Middlesbrough's Dennis F12. Taking up the registration DDC 1, it was assigned to Stockton. In 1991, the number plate was transferred yet again, onto the replacement appliance.

Top Right: *Appliances based on the Ford 'A' series chassis were more often seen in the private and industrial Brigade settings, but Cleveland acquired one in 1980 for operation from Middlesbrough's Marine Fire Station. It was in service for just over ten years and passed to a local industrial Brigade upon disposal.*

Middle Right: *There were two foam tenders in the Cleveland fleet, both based on Dennis chassis. This DF133 dates from 1982 and was based at Grangetown. Later a new slab-sided body was fitted to enclose the foam and water tanks.*
T. Welham

Bottom Right: *Cleveland County Fire Brigade took delivery of two unusual Steyr-Daimler Puch Pinzgauer six wheel drive 'multi-function off-road' vehicles in 1991 for service in the Grangetown and Coulby Newham districts.* T. Welham

A long line of Dennis deliveries commenced in 1976 with five recently introduced R130 models, the only ones in the north-east. One of the batch was specially equipped to carry the wheeled escape at Saltburn and this appliance was the last operational escape carrying appliance to operate in the north-east of England. It was severely damaged after overturning in a road accident, but returned to service after being rebuilt. Latterly it operated as a water tender ladder when the wheeled escape was replaced by a 45ft light alloy Lacon ladder. Fortunately the historic appliance has survived for future restoration and preservation. Two more unusual appliances for the north-east were delivered at the end of the 1970s.

First was a Range Rover-Carmichael Commando 6x4 rescue tender, the sole Range Rover fire appliance in the north-east apart from three similar units used at Newcastle Airport. The impressive six wheel drive rescue tender operated out of Hartlepool's Stranton fire station for almost 15 years before being sold in 1990. It was replaced by a full sized emergency tender. Three years later a small pump on a three-litre petrol engined Ford 'A' chassis with G&T 'Attack' bodywork was delivered for the Marine Station at Middlesbrough, principally for meeting the access and weight restrictions at Middlesborough's main shopping precinct area. For the next 15-years, until 1995, all pump deliveries were based on the steel cabbed Dennis RS and SS chassis or their successors with bodywork by Dennis Bros or John Dennis Ltd. This made for a very standardised fleet, although the special appliances provided some interesting alternatives.

In 1980 a new Dennis F123 chassis was purchased for which G&T Fire Control of Gravesend were contracted to remount the 1962 Merryweather 100ft ladder from Middlesbrough's AEC appliance. The old chassis was disposed of through the auctions at Maltby, after having been partly converted into a transporter by Brigade Workshops personnel for the prospective purpose of recovering broken down Brigade vehicles. This was the last turntable ladder in the Brigade; all the future deliveries were hydraulic platforms or aerial ladder platforms (ALP), commencing with a former demonstration model Shelvoke & Drewry WY-Carmichael 72ft hydraulic platform with booms by Swedish manufacturer Bronto, the first of its type in the country, it operated from Stranton until August 2000.

Above: *This smart looking Dennis SS135 emergency tender of Coulby Newham only had a short existence as it was written off in a road accident in 1990 after just five years of service. It carried an incorrect registration number for several years.* T. Welham

In 1982 a new Dennis DF133 foam tender was delivered for Billingham. Originally this appliance, and a similar Saxon-bodied example delivered in 1986 for Grangetown, had bodies with exposed tanks but were both later re-bodied locally, re-appearing with additional slab sided body panels, concealing the tank. A new Dennis SS135 emergency tender was delivered in 1985 for the new Coulby Newham Station.

Resplendent with its white painted front, the appliance had the distinction of operating for almost five years with slightly incorrect registration plates. These were later replaced by the correct ones, but it was prematurely written off in a road accident. The development of the locally-designed 'Cleveland' emergency tender delivered to Hartlepool in 1990, was on a Dennis DFS237 chassis and featured extending rear body compartments.

Despite the extensive development and design studies that went into the novel approach, the idea was not as appropriate as envisaged and after three years the extending body sections were welded closed and two years later, local company Tyne Tees Coachworks of Coundon rebuilt the body to incorporate additional command support facilities. As well as the full size emergency tenders, for a small period there were three reserve vehicles, all on Ford Transit chassis and based at the three stations that operated emergency tenders. Some years later, the three emergency tenders were assigned individual specialist roles of Rescue/Heavy Rescue, Rescue/Line, Rescue/Chemical and Rescue/Fire Ground Command & Control.

An interesting purchase in late 1986 was a surplus former South Shields Fire Brigade Dodge 50ft hydraulic platform, that was acquired from Tyne & Wear Metropolitan Fire Brigade with the intention of mounting the booms onto the fireboat *Cleveland Endeavour*, to replace the vessels existing platform equipment. The idea was not proceeded with and the appliance was sold twelve months later. Appliances of foreign descent first appeared in the fleet in 1986 with the arrival of a Scania tractor unit for towing the Brigade's 4,000 gallons foam tank trailer that reposed in the yard at Billingham. A beaver tail flat platform trailer was also part of the equipment. Two more Scanias followed in 1988 and 1991, both fitted with Simon Engineering aerial ladder platforms. The second of the pair took the old Middlesbrough registration DDC 1, by now on its third issue.

Below: *The first and only production model of the 'Cleveland' emergency tender, shown at Hartlepool just after delivery in 1990. The two rear compartments could be extended backwards individually to gain access to equipment stored along the centre-line. It later had a very substantial re-build.*

Other appliances of overseas origin appeared in 1991 with the delivery of two unusual Austrian built Steyr-Daimler Puch Pinzgauer six-wheel drive 'multi-function off-road' vehicles. They were assigned to Billingham and Coulby Newham. The angular Dennis RS and SS pumping appliances continued to be delivered, with small batches being received in most years between 1980 and 1995. In all a total of 36 such appliances were placed into service in Cleveland.

In late 1995 the first of three Dennis Sabre water tenders arrived for Thornaby, Middlesbrough and Stranton fire stations. They were followed by a further three in 1997, the second batch having coachwork supplied by Excalibur. By this time a slight change occurred with the Brigade title, from henceforth it was Cleveland Fire Brigade, without the 'County' in the title. A complete change occurred in the fleet in 1998 when Scania/Emergency-One pumps were ordered and between this time and 2002, a total of seven were received. From here onwards the base colour of the appliances was changed from the deep red to vermilion, a rather bright orange-red colour.

Above: *The most recent deliveries to Cleveland and other north-eastern Brigades are Dennis Sabres bought under the aegis of the North East Strategic Partnership Board. This 2003 model, based at Middlesbrough still has a liberal amount of white to contrast with the traditional red livery.* T. Welham

Interesting specialised appliances continued to be ordered commencing with a Dennis DFS241 rescue tender. This featured an Atlas AS80.1 hydraulically-operated crane. After the Scania water tenders appliances on Dennis chassis became prominent, again prompted by a unique purchasing agreement under the auspices of the North East Strategic Partnership Board. This saw the four north-east fire brigades enter into a joint ordering scheme to purchase a total of 34 Dennis Sabre water tenders for delivery over three years commencing in 2003. This interesting arrangement saw almost identical appliances, slightly tailored to the individual Brigade in the areas of equipment and ladder stowage being allocated to the four brigades and resulted in a new degree of standardisation.

DURHAM AND DARLINGTON
FIRE & RESCUE AUTHORITY

Durham and Darlington Fire & Rescue Authority can trace its roots back to 1948 when Durham County Fire Brigade was formed following the disbandment of Britain's wartime nationalised fire services. The fleet was anything but standardised, even considering the NFS appliances that formed part of the new Brigade's establishment. Many pre-war appliances were inherited by the new County Fire Brigade and ranged from open topped Albion Greenwich Salamander appliances of Chester-le Street and Consett, to Dennis Braidwood appliances of Stockton and Billingham and the equally popular, Leylands that were originally supplied to Durham City and Stockton.

The remainder of the fleet consisted almost wholly of Home Office issued NFS appliances based on Austin, Bedford and Fordson chassis. A total of 52 former NFS appliances were inherited. Some of them were rebuilt by the Home Office Workshops at Wakefield, reappearing as modern composite limousine water tenders. Also inherited were three former London Fire Brigade Braidwood machines, which were transferred into the County during the war and a former City of Exeter Albion Merryweather turntable ladder that operated from Stockton.

Below: *Austin auxiliary towing vehicles formed part of the stock of most early post-war fire Brigades, some of them remaining in service until the late 1960s. This one at Darlington is hitched to a Coventry-Climax trailer pump.* B. Clayton collection

Top Left: *Darlington Fire Brigade's second post-war appliance was the ubiquitous Dennis F12, their sole example of which is pictured whilst pumping during an incident at North Road in 1969. All of the Darlington fleet were characterised by '999' registration numbers.*

Middle Left: *Post-war, Darlington operated two Commer appliances. The second model was supplied by Carmichael & Sons of Worcester. Upon being declared surplus, it passed to Teeside Airport where it was pictured on the apron in 1970.*

Bottom Left: *The last appliance ordered by Darlington Fire Brigade was an ERF water tender escape with HCB-Angus bodywork. Apart from Saltburn's Dennis, this was the last escape-carrying appliance to be delivered to one of the north-east Brigades. Two years after delivery the appliance was encompassed into the Durham fleet, in whose livery it was photographed back in 1978. A. Smith*

The new Brigade started life with a total of 26 fire stations and approximately 72 appliances in a County that, at the time, stretched from the south bank of the River Tyne to the north bank of the River Tees, but excluded the Boroughs of Gateshead, South Shields, Sunderland, Darlington and West Hartlepool. These all retained separate existences, although Gateshead was later amalgamated with Newcastle-upon-Tyne.

The supply of new fire appliances was then controlled by the Home Office, which placed a number of contracts with fire engineering and chassis builders and then offered the completed appliances on a strict priority basis, to where the greatest need existed. In Durham's case, the first new appliances were provided at the behest of the Home Office when, in 1950, two new Commer water tenders with bodies constructed at the Home Office Workshops at Wakefield were delivered for operation from Hebburn and Durham. The pump was a demountable Morris-Sigmund type with a similar trailer mounted unit towed behind. In the following year, three more Home Office allocations were received, the first being another pair of Commers, but with coachwork by James Whitson of West Drayton, Middlesex; a company renowned for the construction of passenger coaches. The pumping equipment was the same as the previous Commers and all of the above four appliances remained in service until the mid-1960s. The final delivery of the initial allocation was that classic of all appliances, a Rolls Royce-powered Dennis F12 pump escape, the sole example to operate with the Brigade.

All of this appliance's operational life was at Hebburn, where it served for almost 20-years until being relegated to the training school for use by recruit firemen. In 1951, the final pair of Home Office allocated appliances were delivered, both based on the Leyland Comet normal-control chassis. Hampshire Car Bodies built these appliances but, for the first time, the machines featured built-in Dennis pumps. One was later adapted to carry a Merryweather 50ft alloy extension ladder.

Standardisation did not really occur for several years; indeed during the first three years of the Brigade's existence, three different chassis makes and four different body styles were purchased. The first appliances to be replaced by these new deliveries were the pre-war, open-topped appliances; although two of them, the former Durham City Leyland Braidwood and Bishop Auckland Dennis Light Four motor pumps soldiered on until the late 1960s as training appliances at Framwellgate Moor, Durham in company with Stockton's Leyland limousine pump escape.

In 1951 two more Commers were delivered, these ones featuring light alloy bodywork designed and produced by Alfred Miles & Sons of Cheltenham, which had pioneered the use of aluminium, alloys in aircraft assemblies. These were the most modern of the early post-war appliances and featured several innovations such as high vision wrap around windscreens, jack-knife cab doors and roller shutter locker covers.

Top Right: *Durham City Fire Brigade took delivery of this Leyland Braidwood motor pump in 1939. Inherited by Durham in 1948, it remained in the fleet until 1970 as a training appliance. Thus it gained the distinction of being the last Braidwood-styled appliance in service with any of the north-eastern fire Brigades.*

Middle Right: *This classic 1941 Leyland limousine pump escape, with brass adornments and a Merryweather 60ft steel escape was ordered by Stockton UDC Fire Brigade during the war. Transferred to Durham County Fire Brigade in 1948 it remained with the Brigade as a training school appliance until sold in 1971.*

Bottom Right: *Both Northumberland and Durham inherited a number of Fordson and Austin appliances with this kind of configuration, which were precursors of the modern water tender. As can be seen they were basically lorries with a crew cab, water tank and demountable light pump. This particular example is based on a Fordson 7V chassis.* CD&DFRS

Top Left: *Stockton Fire Station operated this unusual Albion appliance with Merryweather 85ft turntable ladder until 1958. Dating from 1934, it was originally delivered new to the City of Exeter Fire Brigade.* CD&DFRS

Middle Left: *Seeing much less action in Durham after 1948 than at its previous theatre of operation, this Albion motor pump was one of three London Fire Brigade appliances transferred to Durham by the NFS. Post-war all three operated from the Brigade's Training School at Felling near Gateshead.* CD&DFRS

Bottom Left: *For over 20-years this control unit provided fire ground communications at large fires within the County of Durham. It was a conversion of a wartime Austin K4 NFS mobile dam unit and remained in service until 1972. It is presently still in existence and stored in the livery and condition of its post-war guise.*

Three more Miles-Commers were delivered the following year and another two in 1953 making a total of seven. In-house conversions produced two interesting appliances, both adaptations of wartime appliances starting with the conversion of an Austin auxiliary towing unit into a smart mobile canteen van. This was followed by an equally interesting conversion of an Austin mobile dam unit into a control unit. Both appliances, stationed at the Brigade Headquarters, gave 20-years of service before being withdrawn in 1972. In between the batches of Commers, two Rolls Royce powered Dennis F8 water tenders were delivered, a smaller version of Hebburn's Dennis F12.

Three further Dennis chassis were delivered in 1954, but featured bodywork by Alfred Miles. Several more batches of Miles-bodied appliances were ordered, but by then Bedford appeared on the scene and these batches were all based on their standard four-ton chassis. As well as conventional water tenders, four of the appliances were equipped for carrying wheeled escapes, which effectively displaced the wartime Fordson escape carriers. Two others were emergency tenders for assignment to the shipbuilding centres of Hebburn and Billingham, replacing two wartime Fordson units. However, these were not disposed of but converted into foam tenders in 1965, thereafter running alongside their replacements for several further years. The establishment in Durham specified two turntable ladders, so as well as the former Exeter City Merryweather appliance, a wartime 60ft hand-operated ladder on an Austin chassis operated from Durham City's fire station.

These were replaced in 1958 and 1962 by new Rolls Royce-powered Dennis F27 vehicles; oddly enough both with different makes of ladder from two German manufacturers and both featuring pumps mounted amidships. The first, assigned to the new Norton fire station, featured a mechanically-operated ladder from Carl Metz, a firm that had considerable success in the pre-war era. Whereas the Durham City vehicle featured hydraulic ladder equipment from the Magirus Company. Norton Fire Station and its appliances (including the Metz vehicle), were transferred to Teesside Fire Brigade upon its formation in 1968 and later passed to Cleveland County Fire Brigade in 1974.

The Metz-equipped 1958 Dennis was sold for further service to Humberside Fire Brigade. The 1962 Magirus-equipped model was then sold to Kent Fire Brigade, so both gave further service in different parts of the country. A slight change of type occurred in the late-1950s, following the introduction of a new small water tender on the Karrier Gamecock chassis by Carmichael and Sons of Worcester. These machines were publicised as the 'most thoroughly tested in the home market.'

Above: *In 1952 two National Fire Service Fordson hose layers were converted into modern emergency tenders for operation in the heavily industrialised areas abounding the Rivers Tyne and Tees. Illustrated here is Hebburn's appliance, the other was based at Billingham. Upon delivery of two new Bedford emergency tenders both Fordson models were converted again, this time into foam tenders. As a matter of interest, a book on Durham's ambulance service during this same period is also available in the Nostalgia Road series. CD&DFRS*

Fitted with Gwynne 500gpm pumps they were shorter, narrower and lower than any other appliance currently in production and had a maximum speed of 60mph. Seven were acquired by the Brigade between 1955 and 1961, the first Carmichael-bodied machines in the County. In 1964, two more Carmichael-bodied appliances were acquired, both on Bedford TK 6 ton chassis for Norton and Hebburn stations. Twenty-three years passed before Carmichael-bodied pumps would again re-appear in the fleet.

Top Left: *The first appliances received by Durham County Fire Brigade after the war, consisted of a pair of large Commer water tenders with bodywork constructed in the Home Office Workshops at Wakefield. The twin flashing lights and the front-mounted searchlight were unusual fitments at the time.* CD&DFRS

Middle Left: *There were five Rolls Royce-powered Dennis F8 appliances in Durham. Three with Alfred Miles coachwork and two Dennis-bodied examples, one of which is pictured here at Chester-le-Street in 1969.*

Bottom Left: *This Commer/Miles water tender was operating from Wheatley Hill when pictured at a major fire at Chester-le-Street in 1969. It was the penultimate one to be delivered and was later converted into a foam tender.*

As the first decade of Durham County Fire Brigade's existence came to an end, the fleet was still considerably varied with a mixture of new appliances on Bedford, Commer, Dennis and Karrier chassis, along with an assortment of wartime appliances that were still awaiting replacement. A variety of coachbuilders had also been used including all the big ones of the time (Carmichael and Miles), as well as the minority builders, the Home Office, James Whitson and David Haydon, which had supplied the two turntable ladders.

A prolific builder of fire engine bodies, post-war (but now sadly defunct) was Hampshire Car Bodies (HCB), later renamed HCB-Angus following a merger with Angus Fire Armour. Following the plethora of Durham's Miles-bodied appliances, HCB were contracted to supply a number of batches of appliances during the second decade. All based on Bedford chassis, these small appliances were very attractive and featured large amounts of polyester/glass in their construction. The whole of the front window surrounds, cab roof and bell housing, engine cowling and instrument panel were manufactured of this material. With one exception, they were all water tenders.

The exception was the first of the batch, a water tender escape sent to Seaham on the coast. Another interesting appliance from the HCB works was a breakdown/recovery vehicle, mounted on a four-wheel drive Bedford RL chassis. It had a crane that was re-mounted from a wartime Bedford QL chassis that had been inherited in 1948. This appliance remained with the Brigade for almost 30-years, and as well as being used for emergencies it was also a useful adjunct to the workshop's department for attending to disabled fire engines.

During the 1960s, HCB-Angus supplied most of the new units, all on Bedford chassis. Between 1964 and 1968 eight of their compact TJ4 design were obtained, with a mix of water tenders and water tender escapes. Thereafter, future orders remained loyal to Bedford and 15 pumps and one emergency tender were delivered on the popular TK and TKEL chassis, fitted with Bedford's 'Hi-performance petrol engine'. The emergency tender was actually an increase in the establishment on this type of appliance, and it served at Fencehouses.

Following the delivery of the last Bedford TK, a complete change in the choice of future appliance makes occurred with the first delivery of Dennis water tenders in many years. This make, with a few minor exceptions was to form the basis of almost all future pumping appliances and commenced with a batch of two diesel-engined Dennis F49 water tenders for Consett and Framwellgate Moor in 1971, the first diesel-powered appliances in the fleet. In addition, five smaller Dennis 'D' water tenders powered by Jaguar 4.2-litre petrol engines and Dennis 5 speed gearbox were bought. Between 1971 and 1982 the Brigade received a total of 40 appliances of this type for front line duties, ensuring a truly standardised fleet of pumps for the first time. In 1971 a new type of appliance was delivered to supplement, but not replace the turntable ladders. This was a Jennings-bodied ERF with an 85ft three-boom hydraulically elevated platform manufactured by Simon Engineering of Dudley, the 'Simon Snorkel'. Darlington Fire Brigade had placed one in service in 1968 and Newcastle & Gateshead Fire Service had been operating one since 1969.

Top Right: *Seven Karrier water tenders were bought by Durham and one example from the last batch is seen on the forecourt at Birtley in 1970. This appliance and its sister were transferred into the Tyne & Wear fleet in 1974.*

Middle Right: *This Bedford RL 4x4 breakdown and recovery vehicle gave just over 30-years of service before it was sold in 1992. The crane was re-mounted from a former NFS vehicle. Its entire service career was spent operating from Framwellgate Moor HQ, where it was pictured in 1968.*

Bottom Right: *A total of eight Bedfords were acquired with this style of HCB-Angus body and comprised of a mixture of water tenders and escape carriers. This example dating from 1967, has been given a 45ft light alloy ladder for training use. This particular example was the last Durham appliance to be delivered with the Francis 'long rolling' siren.*

Top Left: *An unusual view of one of Durham's Bedford TK/HCB Angus appliances. Dating from 1969 the appliance was pictured pumping from the River Wear in Durham City, its wheeled escape having been removed and positioned to give access to the road bridge above.*

Middle Left: *Newcastle & Gateshead, Durham County and Darlington Fire Brigades all operated ERF 85ft Simon 'Snorkel' appliances in addition to their turntable ladders. The cab on these appliances consisted of two identical halves, joined together. This is Durham County's version awaiting instructions early one morning in 1986.*

Bottom Left: *The Brigade's former wartime converted Austin canteen van, was replaced in 1971 by this lengthy new unit based on a Bedford VAM coach chassis. A similar configuration was used for the new control unit built at the same time. The canteen van was the only appliance in the Brigade not to be fitted with radio communication equipment.*

Based for its entire career at Framwellgate, the Simon 'Snorkel' was undoubtedly the biggest and most powerful appliance in the fleet. In 1973 another Simon 'Snorkel' joined the fleet, this one being a smaller 50ft model, mounted on a Dennis F48 chassis complete with pump. It was initially operated as a first line appliance, together with a similar unit carrying a telescopic 'Simonitor' boom. Pumping appliances with hydraulic rescue equipment were envisaged as the appliances of the future and many fire brigades in the north-east experimented with this type of appliance.

As the 1970s approached, there were two former NFS appliances still operational in the County, the canteen van and control unit at Durham. Whilst these did not see much use, they were still an essential part of the establishment. In 1972, they were replaced by two impressive new units based on Bedford VAM coach chassis with bodies by Northern Assemblies Ltd. The control unit featured three compartments with control and conference functions, plus a toilet and washroom. The canteen van could cater for up to 100 people and also featured three compartments with seating for 18 in the central catering area. Both appliances gave just over 20-years service, and after withdrawal the control unit was replaced by a trailer!

Many boundary changes took place in the County of Durham reducing the size of the authority and resulting in consequent changes in the establishment of the Brigade. In 1968 the County of Teesside was formed, and the boundary changes occurring at the time saw Durham's Norton fire station transferred to that new fire authority.

Twelve months earlier, in April 1967 the retained fire station at Hartlepool Headland had been transferred to West Hartlepool Fire Brigade, whilst yet more local government changes in 1974 saw the formation of the Tyne & Wear Metropolitan County. As part of these boundary changes fire stations at Birtley, Chopwell, Hebburn, Swallwell and Washington were all transferred to Tyne & Wear. At the same time Darlington County Borough Fire Brigade lost its individuality and became incorporated into the County of Durham, together with a small part of the North Riding of Yorkshire, although no fire stations were included in the latter. Almost overnight the Durham fleet had diminished by some ten pumps, one emergency tender and one foam tender, not to mention those lost in previous mergers.

Durham did however acquire the appliances of the Darlington County Borough and its sole fire station. It had had an interesting and varied fleet during it's post-war life span, commencing with the delivery of two Commer appliances with bodywork by Whitson and Carmichael, which both ended their days with the airport fire Brigade at Teesside Airport. The life-saving appliance was a Dennis F12. Darlington also operated one of only two turntable ladders mounted on Leyland's unique and revolutionary Firemaster chassis. Delivered in 1961, it replaced a pre-war Dennis 75ft Magirus vehicle and remained in service at Darlington until withdrawn in 1997.

Top Right: *Later batches of Dennis D water tenders, commencing in 1975, featured re-styled front ends. This one, seen at Fencehouses was the second last of the line. Further deliveries, with the odd exception consisted of the reinforced-steel cab DS appliances.*

Middle Right: *Before the new Dennis DS appliances were introduced, three water tenders on the larger SS chassis were delivered. Dating from 1983, illustrated here is one of two examples assigned to Consett. It is pleasing to note that at this stage the Brigade was still specifying an overall red livery and had not succumbed to the change to unpainted aluminium, except for the locker covers.*

Bottom Right: *There has always been a water relay unit in Durham County Fire Brigade's fleet, in later years this was based on a succession of Commer and Dodge appliances. This 'Walk-Thru' version was delivered in 1979. The units carried extra supplies of hose, which could be paid out whilst driving and portable pumps for setting up additional water supplies, especially at farm fires in remote areas.*

Top Left: *Four angular looking Mountain Range-bodied Bedford water tenders were delivered to Durham County in 1984 and allocated in pairs to Seaham and Peterlee. They were the only ones of the type in the north-east and were sold after just ten years of service.*

Middle Left: *The A1M motorway, traversing the County of Durham, prompted the purchase of a Land Rover Defender/Pilcher Greene road accident vehicle/rescue tender in 1987. During its short ten-year career it operated from the stations at Fencehouses and Newton Aycliffe.*

Bottom Left: *Following on from the Dennis D water tenders were several batches of the angular Dennis DS models. One of four Carmichael-bodied examples delivered in 1990 and stationed at the coastal coal-mining town of Seaham, H687 ATN was one of several appliances called to this plastics factory fire at Chester-le-Street in 1991.*

The remainder of the fleet transferred over included Dennis pumps, an ERF 85ft hydraulic platform and the penultimate pump escape to be delivered to any of the north-east brigades, also on an ERF chassis. All the Darlington appliances were instantly recognised by the figures 999 incorporated into the registration plate numbers.

New turntable ladders were delivered in 1983 and 1985 for Framwellgate Moor and Darlington. Both Dennis DF133 Carmichael vehicles with Magirus 100ft ladders, they were followed in 1984 by a one-off batch of four Mountain Range-bodied Bedford water tenders. These were assigned in pairs to Seaham and Peterlee. Apart from these four machines and two Scanias delivered in 1988, all other pumping appliances were of Dennis make although a number of coachbuilders were used including Fulton & Wylie, Carmichael, Emergency One and Excalibur. Certainly as far as the pumps were concerned, a high degree of standardisation was evident. Following on from the Dennis D models came the 7ft wide, short wheel base DS model, specially designed by Hestair Dennis for rural areas. These models featured a steel safety cab with tilt facility.

Durham received their first batch of two in 1985 and ultimately received a total of 19 of them. After these, the new Dennis Rapier water tender (designed from a joint venture between John Dennis Coachbuilders and Dennis Specialist Vehicles) was adapted for the next generation of appliances. By 1996, 15 of these Cummins-engined six-cylinder turbo-diesel vehicles were in service in the county.

Above: *After many years of using Dennis pumps, a series of Scania-based appliances with coachwork by Emergency One were placed into service by the Cleveland Fire Brigade. This one is Stockton's example and is finished in the new vermilion and white livery. In all, seven such appliances were delivered before the Brigade reverted back to purchasing appliances on Dennis chassis in common with the other north eastern fire Brigades.*
T. Welham

Right: *From 1971, most pumping appliances in Durham's fleet were Dennis-based commencing with a long line of Jaguar-engined 'D' types. One of the four 1973 examples is pictured here at Framwellgate Moor in 1988; it was sold in 1990. Forty-one examples of this type of appliance were purchased by the Brigade between 1971 and 1982 before the angular steel-reinforced DS151 model was introduced into service in 1985.*

Above: *This smart Dennis R 130 water tender escape had the distinction of being the last escape carrying appliance to be delivered to any of the north-eastern fire brigades. Delivered in 1976 to Cleveland Fire Brigade's Saltburn Fire Station, it later operated with a 45ft light alloy ladder in place of the wheeled escape. Fortunately this appliance is one that has been subsequently preserved and restored to its original condition as illustrated in this photograph.*

Left: *The last appliance ordered by Sunderland was this smart-looking ERF/ HCB-Angus water tender ladder. In addition to its impressive cab, it was the only one in the region with twin headlamps. However, delivery of this vehicle did not occur until after the local government reorganisation of 1974 and the appliance therefore never appeared in Sunderland livery. It is photographed in service with Tyne & Wear at Washington in 1976.*

Above: *For the latter part of the 1960s, AEC adopted the new Ergomatic cab, which is pictured here on FCU 542F. Three of these smart AEC TGM-Merryweather appliances saw service with north-eastern fire brigades. Sunderland bought one in each of 1967 and 1968 and South Shields acquired this example in 1968. Pictured at the Brigade's headquarters station in Keppel Street, following disposal by Tyne & Wear Fire Brigade, the body was ignominiously removed and the machine converted into a recovery vehicle by a local coach firm.* Ian Moore

Right: *Northumberland's Volvo's were amongst the smartest in the country and featured many additional embellishments, notably the increasingly rare addition of chrome wheel centres. These two Angloco appliances were the first in the fleet and, apart from an example delivered to Dyfed Fire Service in Wales, they remained a rare variant.*

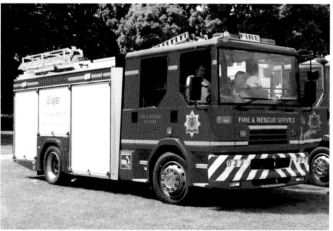

Above: *The oldest appliance to be inherited by Tyne and Wear Metropolitan Fire Brigade, was this canteen van from the South Shields Brigade. It features a Morris Commercial chassis, which whilst popular in all kinds of applications was not a big hit with the fire services. It had been a former Civil Defence ambulance, which South Shields acquired on permanent loan in 1965. It was later preserved and converted into a drop-side lorry.* Ian Moore

Left: *The North East Strategic Partnership Board saw the four north-east fire brigades cumulatively purchase Dennis Sabres, initially with Excalibur bodies. Northumberland's contribution was for eight appliances to be delivered in 2003 and 2004. However, the demise of the body builder saw the remaining two orders for Northumberland contracted out to an alternative manufacturer. Note the advertisement for Draeger breathing apparatus sets on the locker cover.*

Special appliances continued to be replaced and some interesting variants appeared such as a coach-built Land Rover rescue tender with Pilcher-Green body for Fencehouses. This was a 'first' for the Brigade, although regular short wheel base Land Rover utility vans had been used for general purpose duties for many years. In 1992 the title of the Brigade was changed to Durham County Fire and Rescue Brigade.

In amongst the batches of Dennis appliances, Volvo made an appearance in 1994, when the Brigade purchased an FL6 prime mover with multi-lift capabilities for conveying various modules or pods (such as a breathing apparatus training chamber). During the same year two other special appliances were delivered; a Special Incident Unit containing equipment for dealing with chemical spillages, and a purpose-built foam tender carrying 1,800-litres of foam, water/foam monitor and emergency floodlighting equipment. The following year, an interesting new heavy duty wrecker based on a Volvo FL10 chassis was delivered for Bishop Auckland fire station.

This appliance was equipped with heavy rescue equipment, Tirfor winches, a special trolley for conveying equipment along

Above: *Durham County received its first Dennis Rapier appliance in 1992, one of the first customers for this new kind of appliance. Carmichael did the coachwork for the first three batches and illustrated is an example from the initial batch. It operated initially from Darlington.*

railway lines and a rear-mounted hydraulic crane with a 20-tonnes under-lift capacity. The delivery of this appliance saw the withdrawal of the last former Darlington appliance, a Holmes 750 wrecker mounted on a Dennis Maxim chassis. In 1996 and 1999 both Dennis turntable ladders were replaced by the increasingly popular Volvo-Carmichael Bronto 32m aerial ladder platform appliances.

In 1997 the Durham and Darlington Brigades integrated to form a combined fire authority resulting in another change of title, this time County Durham and Darlington Fire and Rescue Brigade. From the 1970s onwards Dennis makes proliferated in the County and continue to do so for the short term at least, with the arrangements for further Dennis Sabres agreed through the auspices of the North Eastern Strategic Partnership Board.

NORTHUMBERLAND FIRE & RESCUE SERVICE

This Brigade started its life with a small collection of pre-war appliances inherited from various Urban and Rural District Councils, some of which were of the open-topped Braidwood-style. These included an impressive Dennis Big Four pump escape from Wallsend, a diminutive Dennis Ace at Hexham and a Bedford from Alnwick. Three Leylands were also included in the fleet, all of the enclosed limousine type that had originally been ordered by the UDCs at Blyth, Gosforth and Newburn. Gosforth's appliance was unusual as it was formerly constructed as an open-bodied Braidwood vehicle, but following an accident during the war the lime green coloured machine was rebuilt in the Home Office workshops at Newcastle and reappeared as a modern limousine. All of these appliances remained at their original pre-war locations and were supplemented by a fleet of 'wartime issue' standard fire appliances on Austin and Fordson chassis, handed over by the NFS.

Above: *This combination of limousine and Braidwood-style body was unusual and is seen on a 1937 former Newburn Urban District Council Leyland motor pump. This was the last of the pre-war council appliances to be disposed of and lasted in service for almost 30-years.* NRFS

The pre-war appliances were withdrawn fairly early on in the Brigade's existence, and it was left to the former National Fire Service standard appliances to provide fire cover for the county. In this period, the most common of these ex-NFS vehicles was the ubiquitous auxiliary towing vehicle based on the Austin K2 chassis. This was basically a box van type personnel carrier towing a trailer pump. A post-war conversion kit was obtainable from the Home Office, enabling the appliances to be fitted with a small water tank and hose reel pump. With this modification having been undertaken, these appliances served the rural part-time/retained stations, for several years, the last one not being withdrawn until as late as 1968.

Whole time stations such as Berwick and Whitley Bay were equipped with Austin K4 and Fordson escape-carrying units, which were later fitted with Barton front-mounted pumps. The remainder of the pump fleet, with one exception, were either Fordson or Austin mobile dam unit conversions. They were basically flat platform lorries with a crew cab, water tank and demountable pump. The exception was a Fordson WOT6 four-wheel drive water tender at Alnwick, the only water tender in the early post-war fleet, yet the forerunner of future water tender developments. Whilst the original establishment proposals called for a number of emergency tenders for the fleet, none of the Fordson appliances inherited were adapted for this role. In fact, Northumberland was never a stronghold for special appliances; that is those other than standard pumping appliances. Even down to this day, the situation remains as such.

Very early on it became clear that an appliance and fire station replacement programme was an urgent necessity. Yet new fire appliances were in decidedly short supply, as were the choices available. In 1950 Northumberland was approached by the Home Office and offered the seventh of a new breed of Commer water tender with coachwork by James Whitson of West Drayton, Middlesex. The offer was taken up and this appliance became the first new vehicle to be placed into service by the Brigade. It was quickly followed by another Commer appliance, but this time with coachwork by Carmichael & Sons of Worcester. It was these two appliances that prompted the choice of Commers as a basis for the post-war fleet.

Top Right: *A long way from home, the former Hexham UDC Dennis Ace motor pump is pictured at Wallsend in 1952, whilst on reserve duties. The neighbouring Tynemouth Fire Brigade once had a similar model, making them the only two of this type to operate in the north-east region.*

Middle Right: *Gosforth's interesting Leyland limousine with cherished number plate originally started life as an open-topped Braidwood appliance painted in the Urban District Council's lime green livery. Following a road accident during the war it was rebuilt into the form illustrated.*

Bottom Right: *Austin ATV models formed the nucleus of appliances at Northumberland's retained stations and illustrated here is a typical example of one that has undergone some post-war additional fitments; including the fitting of a small water tank and hose reel. The pump was mounted on a trailer and towed behind.* NFRS

Top Left: *Wartime Fordson escape-carrying units were also frequently part of the inventory of many post-war Brigades. Originally, many of them towed trailer pumps via an elongated tow bar to clear the escape, until the Home Office offered Barton front-mounted pump conversion kits; one of which has been fitted to this Berwick-upon-Tweed appliance (Berwick incidentally being England's northernmost town).* NFRS

Middle Left: *Northumberland's last trailer pump was not withdrawn until the early 1970s. Of Morris-Sigmund make, it is pictured at Whitley Bay in 1970, unhitched from its prime mover, the Carmichael Commer formerly at Berwick.*

Bottom Left: *This smart Carmichael-bodied Commer water tender was the second appliance to be delivered to the newly formed Northumberland County Fire Brigade. It was allocated to Berwick-upon-Tweed. The mix of hinged and roller shutter locker covers was an unusual configuration at the time.* NRFS

A third option came when former aircraft designers Alfred Miles of Cheltenham, Gloucestershire made available a new water tender. First exhibited at the Festival of Britain, this model became the third new appliance for Northumberland and was assigned to Morpeth.

There were then three different styles of Commer appliances in service in the County. So, after a period of evaluation to see which appliance would best meet the needs of the County Fire Brigade, the light alloy Miles water tender appliance was chosen. With its exceptional visibility from the driver's seat it thereafter became the type that would form the basis of the initial appliance replacement programme.

In 1952 Alfred Miles adapted the water tender to accommodate a 50ft wheeled escape, whilst retaining all of the attributes of a water tender; including the four hundred gallons water tank. This multi purpose pump, of which Wallsend fire station received the prototype, also became adopted as part of the fleet standardisation programme. Within a period of twelve years the entire fleet of appliances at the whole-time fire stations consisted of a pair of Commer/Miles appliances, one water tender and one multi-purpose pump. This was undoubtedly standardisation at its ultimate and Northumberland found that this approach gave many advantages.

The ten part-time/retained fire stations, situated in the rural areas of the County such as at Wooler, Rothbury and Haltwhistle also received Miles-bodied appliances, but these were on Rolls Royce-powered Dennis F8 appliances.

This appliance, originally developed by Dennis for the Northern Ireland Fire Authority (a classic in its own right), was selected as the type best suited for the retained stations because of its narrow width. Yet, to keep in line with the remainder of the fleet, Miles bodywork of a style identical to the Commers was specified rather than the Dennis-bodied examples. Six other appliances completed the initial replacement programme. These were hose/personnel carriers based on Karrier four-door cab chassis, with bodywork once again by Alfred Miles.

The original order for the first two of these called for Bedford chassis, but later Rootes vehicles were specified. Originally designated hose/salvage tenders, these six appliances were stationed at sites bordering Europe's largest man made forest at Kielder, which was seen as a 'big risk' in the northern and western regions. They carried 6,000ft of hose; 350ft flaked for 'laying' whilst the vehicle was under way. Trailer pumps were obligatory pieces of equipment in the first two decades and all of the water tenders carried a demountable pump on the rear, added to which they towed a second trailer-mounted unit. Meanwhile the hose carriers, equipped with a small hose reel pump, also towed trailer pumps. The last two new Commers came in 1963 and 1964, and were part of an add-on order that became necessary to equip a new fire station at Ashington when industrial action with the Coal Board's Fire Brigade saw that organisation withdraw from providing fire cover to the area.

Top Right: *Northumberland standardised on appliances based on Commer chassis with Alfred Miles bodywork. They eventually bought a total of 22 variants, including two second-hand vehicles. The first one was assigned to Morpeth in 1951 and was still operating there as a reserve some 25-years later when this photograph was taken. It was the only example to carry an aluminium extension ladder.*

Middle Right: *Northumberland was the 'launch customer' for the Commer-Miles multi-purpose pump, the prototype going to Wallsend Fire Station in 1951. The modern radiator grille belies its age and was fitted in 1968 following accident damage. This was one of the hardest-worked appliances in the Brigade.*

Bottom Right: *Morpeth Fire Station received the Brigade's penultimate Commer multi-purpose pump, which is pictured in the yard at its home station in 1968. These appliances carried 400 gallons of water and were basically water tenders carrying a 50ft escape ladder.*

These last two were bodied by Frank Healey of Gloucester, a company set up by ex-Miles employees. They were of the same pattern as the Miles appliances and virtually indistinguishable, unless one caught site of the maker's plate. This then, was the situation following the completion of the post-war appliance programme. With the exception of the original Carmichael and Whitson Commer water tenders (by then part of the reserve fleet), the entire Northumberland fleet was comprised of a total of 36 machines, all bodied by Alfred Miles. Eight years lapsed before any other new appliances were delivered, although plenty of second-hand vehicles were acquired.

The water tender from Alnwick was declared an insurance write-off in 1967 following an accident, and rather than buy a new replacement that was none standard, two second-hand Commer/Miles water tenders were purchased, one each from Gloucestershire and Warwickshire Fire Brigades. The Warwickshire one was acquired principally for reserve duties but never went into service, being reduced to spares in 1968 to keep the ageing Commer fleet serviceable. The Gloucestershire machine underwent the rear body conversion in line with the existing Northumberland fleet and was placed in service at Alnwick.

Below: *Fire Chief's cars, as they were erroneously thought of, are rare now. This one was operated by the Station Officer at Wallsend and is a 1965 Commer Cob utility van.* Ian Moore

Following the disbanding of the Civil Defence organisations in April 1968, two former Northumberland Auxiliary Fire Service green goddesses were bought. Then, after a period of loan to Newcastle Airport they were repainted in the Brigade's standard red livery releasing the two original Whitson and Carmichael Commers, which were re-assigned to driver training duties.

Before the second generation of appliances commenced construction, there was one other appliance in the Brigade worthy of mention. This former Civil Defence Signals Unit, based on a Ford Thames chassis, was purchased in 1968. It was converted into a 'Combined Emergency Services Control Unit' with communications facilities for the three emergency services. Based at Morpeth the appliance saw very little service before it was withdrawn in 1979 and replaced by a small Ford Transit 'workshops vehicle' that saw equally little service.

During the mid-1960s all the Miles water tenders underwent significant conversions that resulted in the withdrawal of most of the trailer pumps, as they were progressively replaced by lightweight Coventry-Climax pumps housed in a new rear body extension and enclosed by a full-width roller shutter cover. The hose/personnel carriers also got a new lease of life when the six appliances underwent conversion to emergency tenders. These were then equipped with Dual Volt 2kw portable generators, four 500watt tungsten halogen lamps, power cutting tools for vehicle extrication and Tirfor winches. Following these conversions the last of the trailer pumps, of Coventry-Climax and Morris-Sigmund makes were finally withdrawn.

Top Right: *Northumberland was the biggest operator of Miles-bodied Dennis F8 appliances. Seen here Haltwhistle's example has just undergone the rear body conversion to accommodate two Coventry Climax light pumps in place of two Morris-Sigmund pumps, one of which was towed behind.*

Middle Right: *Northumberland received ten Dennis F8-water tenders with bodywork by Alfred Miles for use at the rural fire stations and thus was the biggest operator of this type of appliance. The last of the ten was later acquired by the short-lived Auxiliary Rescue Service, Blaydon and is currently in the process of being restored back to its original condition.*

Bottom Right: *Northumberland's first control unit was a former Civil Defence signals unit, acquired in 1968. Lettered 'Combined Emergency Services Control Unit', it was a joint venture with facilities for all three of the emergency services.*

The next generation of appliances, commencing in 1972 were based on the Ford 'D' series chassis with turbo-charged diesel engines. The order called for a total of 17 Fords to replace the earlier Commer appliances. In order to effect substantial savings in their construction it was decided to have the bodies constructed locally, as it was estimated that the cost would be half of what it would be from existing fire appliance builders.

However, whilst it was a good theory, it did not work out in reality as the contractual delivery dates for the first four appliances fell significantly behind time. This led to the contract being transferred to another firm of coachbuilders, where similar problems occurred. Eventually the contract for the balance was awarded to North East Coachbuilders of Prudhoe, who completed the contract. Fitting out and painting was done in the Brigade's workshops, whilst the pumps were refurbished items from displaced Commer pump escapes.

Above: *The last two Commers that were delivered new to Northumberland were bodied by Frank Healey. Apart from the new front assembly and different roller shutter locker covers, they were identical to the Alfred Miles-built appliances. Both worked out of Ashington fire station as can be seen here with WNL 785.* Ian Moore

The Brigade did not need to replace the entire Commer fleet, as four fire stations and eight appliances were transferred to the Tyne & Wear Metropolitan Fire Brigade in 1974; so several of the retained stations acquired new Ford appliances. The delivery of these appliances marked the end of the wheeled escapes, some of which were sold to London Fire Brigade. It was also the end of the Karrier emergency tenders, as the original whole-time manned Fords were equipped with rescue gear and given the designation of water tender ladder/emergency tender (WrL/ET).

The Fords were smart but austere looking appliances with their unpainted aluminium bodywork and clean roof lines. Consequently, they differed little from one another although some later had the bodies painted red and one example at Cramlington appeared with a deep maroon livery. From 1981-onwards all of the locally-built Fords underwent a re-building programme owing to corrosion problems. During this time the opportunity was taken to redesign the bodywork, giving the machines a slightly more pleasing appearance. The last locally-built Ford appliance was delivered in 1978 and thereafter another five Fords were purchased but with coachwork by established fire engineering companies, the first by HCB-Angus of Totton, Southampton and two batches of two with coachwork by Angloco of Batley, Yorkshire, the last of the batch going operational in 1980.

There was one other locally-built Ford appliance, which was originally ordered as an emergency tender for the new Cramlington Fire Station. Various problems and the facility of the new water tenders to carry rescue equipment led to the appliance not appearing in service until 1980 with the new designation of chemical decontamination unit. It replaced Morpeth's old Karrier emergency tender that had been converted for the same role in 1976. As 1980 dawned, Northumberland's entire front line fleet consisted of appliances based on Ford 'D' Series chassis, thus once again giving the county an entirely standardised fleet. However, a complete change came in 1981 when four new water tenders were ordered from Chrysler on Dodge G13 Commando chassis, successors of the Commer Commando. As Chrysler Dodge were the successors of the former Rootes Group, this was therefore a return to the manufacturer of the first generation of appliances.

Top Right: *Six Karrier hose/personnel carriers operated in the Brigade for affording protection to the large forest around Kielder. They were all later converted into emergency tenders.*

Middle Right: *A line up in the yard at the new Morpeth HQ during the opening ceremony. The two Green Goddesses had been purchased from the Home Office for use as reserve appliances; the ERF hydraulic platform was a demonstrator and no such appliances were ever ordered by the Brigade.*

Bottom Right: *From 1972 to 1979 Northumberland took delivery of a total of 17 locally-bodied Ford D series turbo-diesel water tender ladders with the dual role of emergency tender. The last of the line was assigned to Morpeth.*

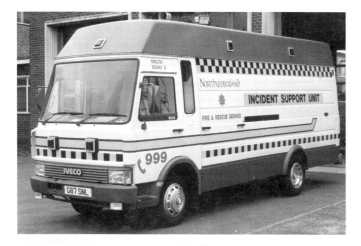

Top Left: *One of the few special appliances to operate in Northumberland was this Iveco "Incident Support Unit', used for dealing with chemical incidents. The radio call sign and emergency telephone number displayed on the side were new innovations for the Brigade.*

Middle Left: *After the locally-built Ford appliances, the next five Fords for Northumberland were all built by established fire engineering companies. The first of four Angloco-bodied water tender ladders was delivered to Morpeth in 1980.*

Bottom Left: *In 1982 four Dodge Commando appliances were delivered with bodywork by Carmichael, the first from this bodybuilder since 1950. Illustrated here is the appliance that was assigned to Hexham in the west of the county.* T. Welham

The Chrysler-Dodge units were powered by Perkins V8 diesel engines with six-speed gearbox with overdrive, and the bodies were by HCB-Angus Ltd. The four appliances were assigned to whole-time stations at Ashington, Blyth, Cramlington and Morpeth and were the last water tender deliveries for seven years.

The next generation was an entirely new concept, foreign-made Volvo vehicles; over the next ten years, all subsequent deliveries were Volvo based. The first two, appearing in 1989, were bodied by Angloco and apart from examples in Dyfed, Wales, these were the only Volvos in the UK to feature the high cab roof designs that characterised these two appliances, which initially operated from Hexham and Ashington fire stations. As well as the Volvos, a number of unusual special appliances were delivered in the 1990s commencing with an Incident Support Unit based on an Iveco chassis for use at incidents involving chemical, radiation and general pollution hazards. Basically the vehicle was a conversion of the standard delivery van and carried extensive gas and radiation monitoring equipment, chemical gas-tight suits, major decontamination equipment and absorbent materials for soaking up chemical spills.

Most unusual though was the all-white livery, specified as a cost cutting measure. Delivered at around the same time was a Volvo FL6 prime mover and multi-lift pod system again in white livery. It came with a selection of demountable modules consisting of a two compartment communications and control pod for establishing fire ground communications, a drop-side lorry module with winch for vehicle recovery and a breathing apparatus training module, which enabled specialised training to be undertaken at retained stations.

Trailer units also appeared, configured with facilities for emergency lighting and forward support, together with a trailer mounted Kawasaki Quad bike for reaching isolated moorlands or forest locations where there might be an incident. Plus, for the first time in Northumberland, a fleet of short wheel base Land Rovers to tow the trailers and also act as personnel carriers and general purpose vans. Over a period of ten years Volvo appliances gradually replaced the Fords and by the end of the century, the entire Northumberland fleet consisted of Volvo-based fire engines.

Great pains had been taken to embellish the appliances and attractive liveries, full-width chrome wheel discs and stylish lettering ensured that the Volvo appliances in Northumberland were amongst the most attractive in the country. After the run of

Volvo's the next generation of appliances were based on Dennis chassis, the first Dennis appliances since the Rolls Royce F8s of the 1950s, and as part of the North East Strategic Partnership Board approval was given for the purchase of a total of eight Dennis Sabre water tender ladders for delivery between 2003 and 2005, six of them having been delivered by the beginning of 2004. Of all the original post-war north-east fire Brigades, Northumberland County, without a doubt was the most standardised of them all.

Below: *Specialised fire engines were never common in Northumberland, but one example was this Ford chemical decontamination unit with locally built bodywork. During its service it operated from Morpeth and Blyth.*

TYNE & WEAR METROPOLITAN FIRE BRIGADE

At the outset of this narrative (the end of World War II), the Tyne & Wear Brigade simply did not exist, and indeed it would not be formed until 1974, following Local Government Reorganisation. As a consequence, this begins with the story of its constituent Brigades that were created when the fire service was de-nationalised.

NEWCASTLE & GATESHEAD JOINT FIRE SERVICE

This joint fire authority was renowned for its unique pre-war livery of deep maroon with vermilion trim, black roofs and liberal black edged silver lining. Six fire stations, Pilgrim Street, Headlam Street, Westgate Road, Gateshead, Team Valley and Walker, plus the fireboat base at Wincomblee were transferred to the brigade after the disbanding of the NFS. The initial fleet was fairly standardised, and based on NFS vehicles and pre-war Leylands consisting of four limousines, one braidwood type and one former Gateshead Borough limousine motor pump.

A second-hand (former Blyth Urban District Council) Leyland limousine was bought from Northumberland County Fire Brigade in 1962, but only for use as a source of spares. The last Leyland was not withdrawn until 1967 having given 30-years of service. New post war deliveries centred predominantly on AEC chassis with a mixture of Regent and Merryweather-Marquis types. However, the first appliance bought was a foam tender based on a Commer chassis, which was bodied by the brigade's own workshop staff. Between 1952 and 1966 all new pumping appliances and the brigade's two turntable ladders were AEC based, the new turntable ladders replacing wartime Leyland appliances, one with a Merryweather 100ft ladder and the other with a 120ft ladder of German Metz manufacture.

Top Left: *Leyland's first limousine turntable ladder was delivered to Newcastle City in 1937. With a height of 120ft it was the second tallest in the country. The venue is the Brigade's HQ station at Pilgrim Street and little has changed since the photograph was taken.*

Bottom Left: *This interesting early post-war view shows three of Newcastle & Gateshead Fire Service's appliances at an exercise at Gosforth. On the right is a Fordson 7V emergency tender inherited from the NFS and on the left a Leyland FK7 cub limousine pump escape, plus the sole Leyland FT Tiger limousine major pump, all from Pilgrim Street.*

Top Right: *One of Newcastle's 'chocolate boxes' seen on Durham Road, Gateshead in 1969. This was the first of three AEC Regent 3 appliances in the Brigade. The original 60ft steel escape has been replaced by a 45ft light alloy extension ladder.*

Middle Right: *To all intents a Merryweather appliance, this AEC Mercury was in fact a product of Angus Fire Armour and ordered through the company's Newcastle office in 1963. Additional embellishments gave it the appearance of a deluxe version of the Merryweather Marquis, one of which is parked behind.*

Bottom Right: *Delivered in 1966, this was the second of two AEC Mercury turntable ladders operated by Newcastle and Gateshead Joint Fire Service. The Brigade was one of the few that still lined out their appliances, in this case, with black edged silver.*

Three AEC Regent dual-purpose appliances were delivered between 1952 and 1953. From then on until 1966 all future pump deliveries were based on AEC Mercury chassis, all but one being produced by Merryweather & Sons. In 1972 a fourth AEC Regent was acquired from South Shields Fire Brigade for use as a driver training vehicle. A slight variation from the AEC allegiance occurred in 1965 with the delivery of a large Dennis F107 emergency tender to replace a converted wartime Fordson hose-laying appliance.

In 1967 they took delivery of the prototype ERF fire engine, a dual-purpose appliance bodied by HCB-Angus. This smart appliance which made its debut at the brigade's centenary celebrations at Newcastle Town Moor featured single track wide profile rear wheels. Subsequently the single rear wheels were replaced by twin wheels and the wheeled escape was replaced by a 45ft light alloy ladder following the brigades policy of withdrawing all of the wheeled escapes in 1968. This pioneering appliance saw ERF successfully enter the fire engine field and the type became the basis of most of the subsequent deliveries with two further HCB-Angus water tenders and two water tenders with 50ft hydraulic platforms arriving in 1971. Sadly the pioneering appliance was later converted into a recovery vehicle for a local coach company and eventually scrapped. An ERF/Fulton & Wylie 85ft Simon 'Snorkel' hydraulic platform was delivered in 1968, this appliance featured a video camera on the platform, from which images could be transmitted to a television receiver housed in one of the lockers.

Top Left: *One of Newcastle's unique Leyland 15-cwt 'mini squirts', which always operated as a pair. As can be seen the cramped cabs necessitated the crews getting dressed in the street, the third rider occupying a seat in the open rear bodywork.*

Middle Left: *Newcastle & Gateshead Joint Fire Service took delivery of the first ERF fire engine. Delivered in 1967, the appliance has twin bells as well as two-tone horns; unusually, the front blinker lights were orange. It became the forerunner of a long line of ERF fire appliances.*

Bottom Left: *Two ERF pump-hydraulic appliances were ordered by Newcastle & Gateshead Joint Fire Service during its closing years. The style of HCB-Angus bodywork was unique to these two appliances, as was the Dayglo striped 50ft booms. This one later became an insurance write off.*

Despite the reasonable degree of standardisation there were some unusual vehicles in the fleet notably the two short lived 'mini squirts' based on Leyland 15 (Standard Atlas) chassis built specially for new indoor shopping developments. During their short life span these three-man appliances (on which the third man rode in the open in the back of the vehicle) replaced one conventional pump. They operated from all of the Brigade's stations during their evaluation trials, following which it was determined that the concept was not viable so both of them were sold, after a spell as general purpose vehicles. They were the last appliances in the city to be delivered in the maroon and red livery.

Two Ford D series appliances were delivered in 1968 and 1969, the first a locally-built emergency/salvage tender that was finished in a gaudy yellow, red, black and white livery. This Gateshead-based vehicle replaced a 1939 Bedford appliance and its receipt was to mark the death knell for the traditional maroon livery. The second Ford was a Hi-Expansion foam tender, finished in an overall red livery and from henceforth no more appliances were ordered with the maroon livery. In fact some of the existing fleet was repainted red, commencing with the prototype ERF. The final delivery, received at the end of 1973 was a Dennis F109 water tender, the first Dennis pump to operate in the city for over fifty years. This appliance became the precursor of the initial deliveries of pumps ordered by the Tyne and Wear Metropolitan Fire Brigade to which Newcastle and Gateshead Joint Fire Service and its four remaining stations was incorporated on 1st April 1974.

There were two fire stations in the Borough of South Shields and in common with other Brigades, their pre-war fleet comprised of an assortment of ex-National Fire Service appliances, one pre-war Leyland Braidwood motor pump plus an estuarial type fire boat. The Borough's allegiance was to AEC appliances with Merryweather fire equipment, and (with one exception) all post-war deliveries were of these types. They commenced with a pair of AEC Regent dual purpose machines delivered in 1951 and 1953 prompting the disposal of a pre-war Fordson appliance, which was sold to Hampshire Fire Service who wanted the front mounted pump. Between 1957 and 1968 a further six AEC-Merryweathers were delivered, based on the Mercury chassis and included a smart combined emergency/salvage tender that also had facilities for use as a fireground control vehicle.

In 1966 a smart foam tender was ordered to cover the new oil storage tank farm at The Lawe, on the banks of the River Tyne. For some years South Shields Fire Brigade had the distinction of having the oldest appliance in the region, a Morris Commercial canteen van, which had been converted from an ex-Civil Defence ambulance. The last appliance delivered, a complete change from previous makes, was a Dodge water tender with 50ft hydraulic platform. On April 1st 1974 the Brigade was incorporated into the Tyne & Wear Metropolitan Fire Brigade.

Top Right: *The first new appliances ordered by South Shields comprised of a pair of AEC Regent III dual-purpose diesel machines with Merryweather fire engineering. The second of the two, seen at Keppel Street in 1968, has the large roof-mounted horn for the Harvin electrified bell system.*

Middle Right: *Coach-built foam tenders were never very common, but the construction of an oil depot at The Lawe was a good enough reason for South Shields to buy one. Like the rest of the fleet, a Merryweather-engineered AEC Mercury appliance was the type chosen for delivery in 1966.* Ian Moore

Bottom Right: *After almost two decades of AEC appliances, South Shields ordered a Dodge/Jennings vehicle with 50ft Simon hydraulic platform. This was the last appliance to be ordered by the Brigade and was later sold to Cleveland County Fire Brigade, in order for the booms to be remounted onto their fireboat.*

SUNDERLAND FIRE BRIGADE

At one time the town of Sunderland had the distinction of being the largest shipbuilding centre in the world. Until the mid 1960s it operated from two fire stations, Dun Cow Street in the town centre, and Fullwell on the north side of the River Wear. By the time of the incorporation into Tyne and Wear, a further two fire stations had been constructed to cover the expansion of the town at Grindon to the west and Ryhope to the south, almost on the County Durham border. Three pre-war appliances were returned to Borough ownership following the disbanding of the National Fire Service, one being a locally-built Bedford emergency tender/wireless, the only appliance to carry a two-way radio at the time and two Leyland limousine appliances, one equipped with a former horse-drawn Shand Mason wheeled escape.

Above: *Sunderland Fire Brigade received this forward control Bedford TJ chassis, which was bodied by Alfred Miles as an emergency tender in 1960. Both West Hartlepool and Durham County Council fire brigades ordered similar kinds of appliances.*

The first new appliances delivered were based on Dennis chassis, with one F7 model being delivered in 1950 followed by two F12s. The first example was later sold to Sunderland's Usworth Airport, where it operated as the crash tender for many years. Sadly an abortive preservation attempt saw the appliance finally being reduced to spares and scrapped. After the Dennis acquisitions, the Brigade standardised for some years on Merryweather-Marquis vehicles mounted on AEC chassis with four examples being placed in service between 1958 and 1965.

The Brigade's turntable ladder was also based on an AEC Mercury chassis and replaced a wartime issued open cab Leyland TD7-Merryweather type, identical to one used in South Shields. The special appliances were based on Bedford chassis and consisted of a Miles-bodied emergency tender delivered in 1960 and a locally-built Bedford TK foam carrier in 1963, which replaced a wartime Austin K2 auxiliary towing vehicle conversion. The last AEC appliances were a pair of TGM-Merryweather pump escapes delivered in 1967 and 1968.

From thereon, a relative newcomer to the fire engine scene, ERF of Sandbach, Cheshire, became the chassis of choice. The first example, a water tender was delivered in 1971, followed the year after by a dual-purpose appliance fitted with a Merryweather 50ft wheeled escape; both of which were bodied by HCB-Angus. This machine only carried the wheeled escape for a very short time and was the last escape-carrying appliance to be delivered to any of the Tyne & Wear constituent Brigades.

In 1973, an emergency tender, based on an example previously delivered to Rochdale Fire Brigade entered service. It was quite unusual for Sunderland, in that it featured a white painted front and white cab doors. The last appliance to be ordered by the Brigade (and in fact delivered after the 1974 merger) was the Brigade's fourth and last ERF. This was again an HCB-Angus-bodied water tender, but it was destined never to carry the Borough's coat of arms.

Top Right: *Sunderland's powerful Leyland FT limousine motor pump operated from Fullwell in the post-war era. It was one of three pre-war appliances inherited at the Brigade's formation. It remained in service until 1963, after which it saw further use as a breakdown recovery vehicle at the Three Mile Garage, Gosforth.* D. Barker

Middle Right: *Three Rolls Royce Dennis appliances were delivered to Sunderland Fire Brigade in the early post-war years. The second example, an F12 major pump is pictured on the forecourt at Dun Cow Street in 1965.* D. Barker

Bottom Right: *Throughout Britain, every fire brigade was compelled to operate an Auxiliary Fire Service for deployment in times of war; for which the Home Office allocated a series of standard fire appliances. One of the types, a Commer Superpoise transportable water unit, carrying rafts and portable pumps, was based at Fullwell. The AFS appliances were finished in a dark green livery with red lettering (see the author's forthcoming book on the AFS fleet).*

TYNEMOUTH FIRE BRIGADE

Tynemouth Fire Brigade, as the name suggests, was situated at the mouth of the River Tyne, on the north side. The area was very compact and consisted principally of the town of Tynemouth and the industrialised area of North Shields on the banks of the river. To the east was the North Sea and bordering the landward side was the County of Northumberland.

Apart from the war years, there was only one fire station which was attached to the police station in the town centre at North Shields. This station was replaced by the second and present station at Preston Road, a mile from Northumberland County's Whitley Bay Fire Station. In the pre-war motorised era the Brigade only had two motors, *Gascoigne*, a Morris Belsize pump escape delivered in 1917 and a Dennis Ace motor pump delivered in 1937.

Above: *Tynemouth Fire Brigade was the first in the Tyne and Wear area to feature an appliance with unpainted aluminium bodywork, a distinction that was not surpassed for many years. Based on a Bedford TK chassis, the appliance was ordered as a foam tender but also had provision to be used as a conventional pump when required.*

With a small area there was no need for a large fire brigade and post-war the fleet comprised of the Dennis Ace and three NFS pumps. Because of enemy bombing attacks and the strategic value of the area due to its commerce and ship-building interests, a diesel-engined Leyland Beaver-Merryweather 100ft turntable ladder was assigned to the area during the war years. Then, following the de-nationalisation of the NFS, between 1948 and 1974 the Brigade bought a total of six new appliances commencing with a pair of Dennis F12s.

The first of the pair of F12s was equipped to carry a 50ft wheeled escape and the second, delivered two years later, was the less common rear pump version although it could carry the escape when required. Both these appliances passed into Tyne & Wear in 1974 having served the Borough well for over 20-years.

Eight years passed before the next new addition to the fleet, a Bedford TK-HCB foam tender. This vehicle was the first appliance in the Tyne & Wear region to feature unpainted aluminium coachwork and retained that record for many years. Although purchased predominantly for use as a foam tender to protect the Esso Terminal at North Shields, it could also be used as a front line appliance when necessary.

They never operated a full size emergency tender but as a compromise a long wheel base Land Rover was adopted for rescue duties, and to contrast it with the red of the Dennis F12s and the silver of the foam tender, this one was painted dark green. The wartime Leyland turntable ladder gave sterling service to the Borough until it was replaced in 1966 by an AEC Merryweather of the type adopted by Newcastle & Gateshead, South Shields and Sunderland. It also made surplus the wartime Leyland Beaver, which was sold to Rentokil. The increasing attendance of the fire brigade at road accidents prompted some thought on the acquisition of an appliance suitable to meet these risks. Quite timely and appropriate came the almost simultaneous disbanding of the Auxiliary Fire Service in 1967 and a consequent surplus of Green Goddesses. In turn this afforded the Brigade the opportunity to acquire one of these Home Office appliances that had been stationed in the town.

Top Right: *Following experiments by Coventry Fire Brigade regarding the most visible livery for fire engines, Tynemouth opted for Coventry yellow when they converted a former Auxiliary Fire Service Green Goddess. This was the only yellow fire engine to operate in the north-east of England.*

Middle Right: *Tynemouth Fire Brigade became the first of the Tyne & Wear constituents to take delivery of a pump hydraulic platform appliance. Bodied by HCB-Angus and pictured in 1971 just after delivery, the appliance later underwent a full re-build following a road accident during which it overturned.*

Bottom Right: *The first appliances bought by the new Tyne & Wear Metropolitan Fire Brigade were based on Dennis F109 and F131 chassis. The fixed roof monitor and twin mirror image FIRE signs are clearly evident on this 1975 model.*

The vehicle was completely refurbished in the Brigade's workshops and re-entered service as a pump/rescue tender. It was then equipped with a wide range of extrication and cutting equipment, hi-expansion foam and all the normal items of fire fighting equipment, enabling the appliance to be utilised at fire calls as well as road accidents. After refurbishment the original Government olive green livery was replaced by striking Coventry yellow. This was the only yellow liveried appliance ever to service in the north east of England.

The last two appliances delivered to the Brigade before the 1974 reorganisation, were both ERFs. They were delivered in 1971 and 1972, some 20-years after the original Dennis F12 machines. The first was a HCB-Angus pump hydraulic platform, the second, a conventional water tender ladder, similar to the Newcastle appliances but with different locker arrangements.

Above: *As well as the Dennis pumps two Dennis F123 turntable ladders with Carmichael coachwork and German Magirus 100ft ladders with detachable rescue cage were delivered to the Tyne & Wear Brigade in 1977 and 1978. One of them, RTN 144S is seen here.*

The notion of fixed roof monitors also applied to this appliance. Two years after the delivery of the ERFs, the County Borough of Tynemouth Fire Brigade faded into oblivion having been absorbed into the fleet of Tyne & Wear. Although the Brigade exhibited the smallest fleet of any of the Tyne and Wear constituents, three of the Brigade's appliances managed to survive long enough for preservation; including the first Dennis delivery, which was retained by Tyne & Wear Metropolitan Fire Brigade and currently resides at Tynemouth Fire Station.

After 1974

Formed on 1st April 1974, the Tyne & Wear Metropolitan Fire Brigade encompassed the former fire Brigades of Newcastle & Gateshead, South Shields, Sunderland, Tynemouth and selected stations from the counties of Durham and Northumberland. Sixty-six appliances, ranging in date from 1948 to 1974, were transferred to the new fire authority. Because of the vast array of different types and makes of vehicle inherited, an early priority was fleet standardisation and to this end the formative years featured new appliances predominantly of Dennis make. This commenced with a series of F109 and F131 pumping appliances in enough quantity to ensure that each of the Brigade's 19 stations operated this type of appliance at one time or another.

The last three to be delivered in 1979 also happened to be the last of a long line of F-Series appliances to be manufactured by Dennis Brothers of Guildford. All featured rearward facing crew seats, fixed roof monitors and reversed illuminating FIRE signs in the front panelling. Four interesting appliances were delivered in the years 1981 and 1982, consisting of a Dennis Dominator bus chassis with Angloco bodywork for a control unit. Specially designed for fire ground control duties it was equipped with a 9kVA generator and featured compartments for telephone and radio communications, a rest room, toilet facilities and even the proverbial kitchen sink in a small catering compartment.

Top Right: *Two Dodge Commando lorries with demountable pods were delivered in 1980. The first, based at Tynemouth is shown with the canteen pod. The other was assigned to the school fire safety programme.*

Middle Right: *The sole Shelvoke & Drewry water tender to be purchased by Tyne & Wear was delivered in 1981 and served most of its career at Hebburn, before being sold for further use with the Irish Civil Defence organisation. The notion of roof monitors low-level blue lights and illuminating fire signs had disappeared by this time.*

Bottom Right: *Shelvoke & Drewry (better known for dustbin wagons) was chosen as the mount for the first of the Brigade's two new foam tender replacements. The liberal fixing of the maker's plates on the front left no doubt as to who supplied the body and foam-making equipment. The appliance was assigned to Whitley Bay.*

Top Left: *At the time of its delivery, this was claimed to be the largest of its type in the country. Based at West Denton, this impressive Dennis Dominator mobile control unit poses on the forecourt whilst waiting fitting out. A crew of two, supported by a pumping appliance crew, manned it.*

Middle Left: *The fourth, and last Shelvoke & Drewry appliance in Tyne & Wear was another emergency tender, but with a specially-shortened body to comply with the appliance room limitations at Wallsend Fire Station. Within months it was returned to the manufacturers for lengthening and later acquired a yellow and red chequered band to the roof front.*

Bottom Left: *After the Dennis F Series appliances, future orders consisted of the steel safety cab 'RS' and 'SS' series appliances. Pictured is one of five 'SS135' Carmichael-bodied appliances delivered in 1986. By this time multi-tone electric sirens had replaced the two-tone horns.*

Delivered during the same period were three Shelvoke SPV appliances to accompany a Shelvoke emergency tender previously delivered in 1977. Of the three new Shelvoke units, one was a water tender purchased for evaluation, the next was a Chubb-bodied foam tender and finally another emergency tender, this one built with special limitations for Wallsend fire station. For some years afterwards the Brigade stayed loyal to Dennis and subsequent pump deliveries and turntable ladders were based on the RS, SS and DF series steel cab appliances bodied by Dennis, Carmichael and Fulton and Wylie. With one exception the entire pumping appliance fleet was Dennis-based.

Volvo-based appliances had been making considerable inroads in direct competition with British manufacturers and in 1987 six Volvo appliances were ordered, one emergency tender and five water tenders, all with bodywork by Fulton & Wylie of Falkirk. For several years after, Volvo became the chassis of choice and several batches from different coachbuilders were delivered between 1988 until 2002. The water tender fleet was reasonably standardised but there was plenty of variety among the special appliances. Two Dodge platform lorries appeared in 1980 as part of a demountable pod system. One unit based at Tynemouth was used to transport a salvage equipment pod, decontamination pod and canteen unit pod and the other was used to transport an educational Fire Safety Unit module. Three unusual GMC 4x4 6.2-litre V8 rescue tenders were delivered in 1988 and 1989 and were equipped to tow a variety of equipment as well as one of the Brigade's two land-based fireboats.

When the appliances were sold after just ten years of service, an obsolete pump was converted into a boat carrier to convey the Tyne-based boat. In 1995 an Iveco-Magirus 100ft turntable ladder was purchased for operation from Fossway fire station followed in 1998 and 1999 by a new type for the area, two Volvo FL10 six wheel chassis with Bronto 32m aerial ladder platforms for Gateshead and Fullwell.

By the time the new millennium dawned, the Tyne & Wear fleet was predominantly Volvo-based with a short run of two small batches of Dennis Sabre water tenders with Excalibur and Emergency One bodies in 1998 and 1999. These were located at stations bordering the rivers Tyne and Wear, where it was envisaged that the 1,000gpm pumps could be put to greater use. There was a return to Volvo again over the following three years and then Dennis reappeared once more with ten Excalibur-bodied water tenders being delivered in 2003 and 2004 to join the six already in service. By then the Brigade was the fourth member of the North Eastern Strategic Partnership Board for joint purchase of appliances.

Above: *Three GMC rescue tenders operated throughout Tyne & Wear from the late 1980s. As well as rescue capabilities the units also had the additional role of towing an assortment of specialised trailers including the fireboats. This Locomotors 'Response' vehicle was stationed at Dun Cow Street, Sunderland.*

With these deliveries it seems appropriate to conclude this brief history of north-east fire engines, and thus logically conclude a 60-year old account that started back with the end of hostilities in 1945. Over the period covered, the individuality and variety of fire engines was replaced by increasing standardisation, made possible following the merger of 1974, which resulted in fewer individual brigades covering larger areas. It is hoped that it will have evoked memories of one of the nation's most illustrious of organisations and serve as a lasting tribute to the men and women that have, and continue to provide a great gift of humanitarian aid to the citizens of the north-east of England.

ACKNOWLEDGEMENTS

The production of this book would not have been possible without the consistent cooperation of the individual Fire Brigades, Chief Fire Officers and personnel that have made their time and resources freely available. Also the important contributors, supporters and life long correspondents and associates who have shared enthusiasm and offered the use of their photographic resources for this history. To the following my sincere thanks are proffered to Ian Moore of Cramlington who has never ceased to share his knowledge and resources during a 40-year association, Trevor Welham from Whitby for the same, Dennis Barker, Brett Clayton, Arthur Smith, *Newcastle Chronicle and Journal*, Durham & Darlington Fire & Rescue Authority and Northumberland Fire & Rescue Service.

Above: *The second batch of Volvo appliances delivered to Tyne & Wear in 1989, featured bodywork by Excalibur. This combination remained for all future pumping appliance deliveries until 1996. Illustrated is Ryhope's appliance after having been re-registered from F262 ORG. After disposal it gave further service to the oil terminal at Sullom Voe in the Shetland Islands.*

Also in this series:

**Volume Three: Fire Engines of the 1950s & '60s.
Volume Six: Fire Engines of North West England
and coming soon, by the same author:
The Auxiliary Fire Service and
Airport Crash Tenders**